Create Your
DREAM ROOM

Awesome projects for the ultimate bedroom makeover

Sophie Splatt

The Five Mile Press

PAPER BUNTING

This simple bunting can be made from any type of paper. Hang your finished bunting across a wall or window to instantly brighten up your room.

Materials: cardboard, decorative paper, string

Tools: ruler, pencil, scissors, hole punch

1. Select decorative paper for your bunting.

2. Using your ruler and pencil, draw a triangle on the cardboard the size you would like your bunting to be. Using scissors, cut this out to use as a stencil.

3. Using your pencil, trace around your cardboard stencil onto the decorative paper.

4. Using scissors, cut your triangle from the paper.

5. Use your hole punch to make two holes in the corners of the top edge of your triangle.

6. Repeat steps 3 to 5 until you have a small stack of triangles.

7. Thread string through the holes in your triangles, until all the pieces are on the string.

8. Hang your bunting, adjusting the position of the pieces along the string as needed.

Try this

- Make your bunting using hearts, circles or feather shapes.
- Draw a letter on each piece of your bunting to spell out your name or a word.
- Make mini bunting to decorate small pieces around your room, such as a pinboard or chalkboard (see page 22).
- Apply glitter to make your bunting sparkle!
- Or use the stencils on page 41 & 42 to make your bunting.

HINTS

- Leave enough string on each end of your bunting so that you can tie it to something in your bedroom. If you can't tie it to anything, get an adult to hammer two nails into the wall and tie each end of the string to a nail.
- For more interesting bunting, use coloured cardboard, the pages from pre-loved picture storybooks, maps, sheet music, paper lace, doilies or old greeting cards.

TERRARIUMS

A terrarium is just like a small greenhouse with its very own climate. With only a few items, including a clear glass container, some tiny plants and friendly figurines, you can create your own miniature world!

Materials: clear glass container, pebbles, horticultural charcoal (purchased at most gardening stores), moist potting mix, plants, moss, small plastic or ceramic figurines

Tools: gardening gloves, kitchen fork, spray bottle

1. Choose a clear container to house your terrarium.

2. Place a small layer of pebbles at the base of your terrarium. Pebbles are important for soil drainage and to avoid damaging the plant roots.

3. Add a smaller layer of charcoal on top of the pebbles. Charcoal will help filter the water and prevent soil from going sour.

4. Put your gloves on. Add the moist potting mix, remembering to leave room for your plants.

5. Remove the plants from their containers. Gently shake the plants to remove excess soil, then tease the roots carefully.

6. Dig small holes in the potting mix using your fork and put in your plants, starting with the largest plants. Don't overcrowd your terrarium – remember, the plants will grow.

7. Pat the soil down around your plants so they won't move.

8. Place pebbles and figurines around your plants (and moss if you are using it) to decorate your landscape.

9. Using a spray bottle, mist your plants with water.

10. Place your terrarium in indirect light, and water using your spray bottle when needed.

moist potting mix

charcoal

pebbles

Try this

- Paint your figurines in gold or silver to give them an other-worldly look.

- If you don't have a large container, use different glasses to make a collection of mini terrariums with individual plants.

- Repurpose small toys to decorate your terrarium world.

HINTS

- Plant either succulents, including cacti, or ferns and moss in your terrarium. Succulents require very little water, and like to live in an open container. Ferns and moss like a more humid environment, so are best suited to a closed container and more regular watering.

- Choose small plants that won't outgrow your terrarium, and a clear container so that you can *see* into your miniature world!

- Remember not to touch the potting mix with your bare hands.

POMPOM RUG

While you will need to make a lot of pompoms to create this rug, they're very easy to do and it will look beautiful on the floor of your bedroom!

Materials: yarns in your choice of colours, woven mat (purchased at any variety store)

Tools: scissors

1. Lay yarn across your fingers (palm up), securing the end with your thumb.

2. Wrap the yarn loosely around all four of your fingers.

3. Continue wrapping until you have a thick bunch of yarn.

4. Slip the yarn carefully off your fingers and cut it free from the ball.

5. Cut a separate length of yarn (around 30cm).

6. Lay the bundle on top of the 30cm piece of yarn so that the hole in the bundle and the yarn both run horizontally.

7. Pull both pieces of yarn up and across the bundle, pulling very tight.

8. Tie a very tight knot so that your bundle is secured in a bow-tie shape.

9. Holding on to the longer lengths of yarn and using your scissors, cut through the loops in your bundle.

10. Fluff the threads of yarn and then trim to create a nice shape. Don't trim the 30cm piece of yarn – you will use this to secure your pompoms to the mat.

11. Repeat steps 1 to 10 until you have a big pile of pompoms in different colours.

12. Use the longer pieces of yarn to tie the pompoms to the mat, knotting them on the underside of the mat. Continue until your mat is completely covered.

Try this

- Create a striped rug by arranging pompoms in single-colour strips.

- Get an adult to cut a large circle from anti-slip matting to create a circular rug.

HINTS

- You can choose any mat or rug for this project as long as it has regular holes in it so that you can tie on your pompoms.

- When making the pompoms, spread your fingers slightly so the yarn doesn't become too tight and is easy to slip off.

- If you have small hands, try winding your yarn around a large wooden spoon, or use the handy pompom maker on page 41.

- The more yarn you wrap around your fingers, the bigger your pompom will be. Try making pompoms in a variety of sizes for a more interesting rug.

Step 2

Step 7

Step 9

DESK DECORATING

Add a splash of style to your desk with these decorating ideas!

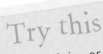
Try this

- Wrap fabric around tins or jars to create stationery holders. Use craft glue to secure the fabric in place.

- Decorate notebooks with patterned washi tape.

- Cover plain exercise book or magazine holders with decorative paper or contact.

- Use any of these ideas with a stack of shoeboxes to create extra storage space.

HINTS

- Use one colour or theme in all your projects to coordinate your desk decorations.

- Label your shoeboxes and folders so you know what each contains. Check out page 47 & 48 for some cool labels you can use on your storage boxes and books.

- Personalise your study space with your own handmade paper, decorated using a simple potato stamp. See page 18 to find out how.

GIANT TISSUE-PAPER POMPOMS

Step 2

Step 4

These impressive pompoms only require tissue paper and string! Make them in different sizes and colours, then hang them high in your room.

Materials: tissue paper, string

Tools: scissors

Step 6

1. Stack between 8 to 10 sheets of tissue paper (sized around 25cm by 40cm).

2. Accordion fold your tissue paper along the short end in strips around 3cm wide until you have a single, folded strip.

3. Tie a length of string around the centre of the strip and knot it. You will use this string to hang your pompom, so make sure that it's long enough.

4. Using scissors, trim the two ends of the tissue paper strip to form rounded edges.

5. Fan your pompom out so that it forms a circle.

6. Carefully peel the first layer of tissue paper on one side upwards towards the centre of the pompom. Repeat until you reach halfway. Turn the pompom over and repeat with the other half. Then repeat the whole process on the other side.

7. Tease the tissue paper until you are happy with the shape of your pompom.

8. Repeat steps 1 to 7 until you have a selection of pompoms.

9. Hang pompoms from the ceiling so they sit at different heights.

Try this

- Layer different coloured sheets of tissue paper to create a multi-hued pompom.
- Once you have folded your tissue paper, use a craft punch to create holes in the rounded edges of the pompoms.
- Why not coordinate your tissue-paper pompoms with your pompom rug? See page 6 to find out how.

HINTS

- Don't worry if your tissue paper tears. Remove the torn paper and tease the rest of the sheets around the tear.
- Pompoms can be made in any size, but smaller ones will maintain their shape more easily.

JEWELLERY ORGANISER

Here's a clever way to organise your jewellery collection that also makes a beautiful display!

Materials: old wooden drawer, paint in your choice of colour, lightweight doorknobs, decorative paper, craft glue, paperclips, two drawing pins, small bowls

Tools: sandpaper, clean cloth, newspaper, paintbrush, scissors, ruler

1. Lightly sand your drawer until the surface is smooth. Use a clean cloth to wipe the excess dust off.

2. Lay down some newspaper to do your painting on. Paint the wooden drawer in your selected colour and leave it to dry. Don't forget to paint both the inside and outside of the drawer.

3. Paint your doorknobs and leave them to dry.

4. Use a ruler to measure the inside of your drawer. Cut a piece of decorative paper to the size of these measurements.

5. Use your craft glue to carefully glue the decorative paper onto the inside of the drawer.

6. Loop paperclips together to form a chain slightly longer than the width of the drawer.

7. Using the drawing pins, fix the last paperclip on both ends of the chain to the top sides of the drawer. Make sure the chain is positioned a few centimetres from the back of the drawer so that it is hanging freely.

8. Glue the doorknobs onto the decorative paper, or ask an adult to help you attach them with screws. The doorknobs should be positioned far enough down from the top of the drawer so that your jewellery can fit on.

9. Arrange the bowls at the base of your drawer.

10. Hang necklaces from the doorknobs and earrings from the paperclip chain. Fill the bowls with bracelets, brooches and rings.

Try this

- Paint each doorknob in a different colour.
- If you can't find a drawer, use a large shoebox. If you don't have doorknobs, use hooks.
- For decorative paper you can use wrapping paper, wallpaper or contact. Anything that will make a pretty backing for your jewellery organiser will work!
- Use old teacups or small glasses to store your rings and bracelets.

HINTS

- Make sure your doorknobs are deep enough to hold a few necklaces.
- Only place light earrings on your paperclip chain.
- Decorate the sides of your organiser with a stencil. See page 33 & 34 for handy stencil templates.

CUPCAKE FAIRY LIGHTS

Make pretty shades for fairy lights using paper cupcake liners. Hang strings across your wall or dangle them from your curtain rail – when you turn them on at night your room will be instantly transformed!

Materials: string of LED fairy lights, cupcake liners (thin paper liners work best)

Tools: small Stanley knife or kitchen skewer

1. Ask an adult for help with this step. Use the Stanley knife to cut a small 'X' shape into the bottom of each cupcake liner. Or, use a kitchen skewer to poke a small hole into each liner.

2. Hang your LED string of fairy lights in the place you want them to be. Then, poke each light globe through the hole in the bottom of the cupcake liner.

Try this
- Experiment with using multi-coloured fairy lights.
- Mix and match liners of different colours, patterns and sizes to create your ultimate display.
- Fold cupcake liners in half and then half again, and again. Then, using scissors, trim the top edge of the liner to form a rounded shape. Unfold and you'll have a pretty flower-shaped liner to use as a shade.

HINTS
- Only use LED fairy lights as these will not overheat, and never leave them on overnight or when you are out of the room. Check with an adult if you are unsure.
- Hang several strings of lights for an impressive effect.

GLITTER WORDS

Sparkle up your bookshelf by spelling out your name with these three-dimensional glitter letters!

Materials: papier-mâché letters (purchased in any craft store), acrylic paint in your choice of colour, clear craft glue, glitter

Tools: newspaper, paintbrush

1. Lay down some newspaper to work on. Paint the sides of your letters in the colour of your choice. Leave to dry.

2. Apply a thick coat of craft glue to the front of one letter.

3. Sprinkle glitter onto the letter until the entire front is covered. Allow to dry.

4. Repeat steps 2 and 3 with each letter of your name.

5. Display your letters on your bookshelf or desk.

Try this

- Spell out other words or cover your favourite numbers.
- You can use the same method to cover other shapes or boxes with glitter.

HINTS

- Make sure you use craft glue that will dry clear. Check the label if you are unsure.
- Glitter will be messy! Lay down newspaper before you begin for an easy clean up.
- If you only want to apply a light touch of glitter, paint both the front and sides of your letter in coloured paint. The paint colour will be visible under your thin layer of glitter.

POTATO-PRINT CUSHION

Sit back and relax in comfort with your very own cushion design, made using the potato-print method.

Materials: large potato, fabric paint, plain cushion cover

Tools: knife, cookie cutters in various shapes, paper towel, newspaper, paintbrush

1. Cut a potato lengthways in half.

2. Use a cookie cutter to press a shape into your potato, then get an adult to help you cut away the potato outside your shape to form a stamp.

3. Blot your potato onto the paper towel to remove excess moisture.

4. Lay down some newspaper to work on. Using your paintbrush, apply a thin layer of fabric paint to the potato stamp.

5. Test your print by pressing the stamp onto a piece of newspaper. You may need to apply more or less paint to get a good print.

6. Once you are happy with your print, lay your cushion cover flat and stamp a pattern onto it.

7. Follow the instructions on your fabric paint to set the paint.

Try this

- Print onto pillowcases, bedspreads or any plain fabrics in your room.
- Use this method with acrylic paint to make coordinated decorative paper to cover storage boxes — see page 8.
- Draw your design onto your potato in pencil, then remove the potato around your shape using your knife.

HINTS

- Simple, geometric shapes work well to form a pattern.
- For best results, use a light-coloured cushion cover and darker paints.
- If you don't have a potato, you can use an apple.

PHOTO DISPLAYS

Here are some creative ways to display photos in your bedroom. Try one or try them all!

Curl photos in glass bottles or jars and display them along a shelf. Look around your house for unwanted supplies. Second-hand shops or trash-and-treasure markets are also great places to find pretty bottles and jars. Decorate the jars with washi tape, ribbons, lace, or tiny strings of bunting.

Remove the backing and glass from a large old picture frame. Hang lines of string across the empty frame, securing the string in place at the back of the frame with masking tape. Peg photos along the string. To coordinate your frame with the rest of your room, paint the frame in a colour of your choice.

Try this

- You can also use all these ideas to display your artwork or favourite pictures from magazines.
- Try printing your photos in mini sizes, or trimming them into different shapes for a cute new look.
- Check out the photo frames on pages 35–38. You can hang these on your strings, stick them on your walls, or use them inside ready-made frames for an extra-special wall display.

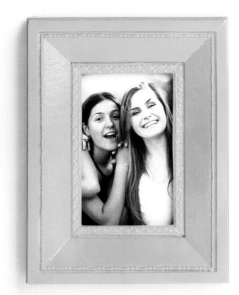

Use mismatched frames painted in a few selected colours to create a photo wall. Or paint them all in the one colour, or shades of the one colour, to really tie your display together.

HINTS

● You can also stick coloured tape along the edges of your photos to create instant borders.

PINBOARD & CHALKBOARD

Transform unused picture frames with these two simple projects! A pinboard is a great way to display your special memories and photos, while your very own chalkboard is great for drawing on, or for leaving yourself reminders.

Materials: two large picture frames (you can repurpose old frames), plywood, chalkboard paint, chalk, pinboard (purchased from any stationery store or variety store), wadding (purchased from any craft store), fabric of your choice, flat drawing pins, elastic, decorative pins

Tools: newspaper, sandpaper, clean cloth, paintbrush, sponge, scissors

To make the chalkboard:

1. Choose a frame for your chalkboard.

2. Lay down some newspaper to work on. Lightly sand a piece of plywood that will fit into your frame (a hardware store can cut plywood to the size you need). Wipe away dust with a clean cloth.

3. Using your paintbrush, cover one side of the plywood with a layer of chalkboard paint. Allow to dry following the instructions on your paint tin, and then apply another layer of paint if needed.

4. Fit the plywood into the picture frame with the painted side facing the front.

5. Rub chalk all over your chalkboard then wipe with a lightly dampened sponge.

HINTS

- If needed, use masking tape along the edge of your plywood and pinboard to fit them to the frames.

- Use a measuring tape or ruler to work out the size of your frame.

To make the pinboard:

1. Using scissors, cut a piece of thin wadding to the size of your pinboard.

2. Cut a piece of fabric slightly larger than your pinboard and lay this over the top of the wadding and the pinboard.

3. Turn your pinboard over. Stretch the fabric tightly and use flat drawing pins to secure the fabric to the frame of your pinboard.

4. Run elastic diagonally across your pinboard to form diamonds and secure it to the edges of the back of the pinboard using flat drawing pins.

5. Where the elastic meets (at the tips of the diamonds), secure to the pinboard using decorative pins.

6. Place the pinboard inside your second picture frame and secure in place.

Try this

- Coordinate your boards by painting your picture frames in the same colour.

- Hang some cute mini bunting at the top of your frames. See page 2.

HANGING HEARTS

This paper sculpture will look super cute hanging from your ceiling as a mobile. Or try hanging it on your door.

Materials: straight branch, paint, string, coloured paper

Tools: sandpaper, newspaper, clean cloth, paintbrush, marker, scissors, stapler

1. Find a straight branch around 75cm long. Ask an adult to help you cut the branch down to size, if needed.

2. Lightly sand your branch. Wipe away any dust with a clean cloth.

3. Lay down some newspaper to work on. Paint your branch in your choice of colour and leave it to dry.

4. Using your marker, draw a heart on a piece of newspaper – make the width of the heart around 65cm, and the length about 50cm. Cut out the heart. You will use this as a template for positioning your coloured hanging hearts.

5. Working on a flat surface, position your branch about 10cm above the top of the newspaper heart. Tie lengths of string at intervals of around 6cm along the branch. Cut each piece of string slightly below the bottom edge of the outline of the heart.

6. To make the hanging hearts, cut strips of coloured paper about 10cm long and 1.5cm wide.

Step 7   Step 8

7. Starting at the top centre of your newspaper heart, place two pieces of coloured paper on either side of one piece of string and staple the string between the two pieces on the bottom edge.

8. Fold each piece of paper out and down, then staple the string between the two pieces again at the bottom to form your heart shape.

9. Repeat steps 7 and 8 as you work your way around the newspaper heart shape.

10. When you have stapled all the hearts on, adjust them if needed by pulling them up or down along the string.

11. Get an adult to help you hang your mobile in your room.

HINTS

- To make a symmetrical newspaper heart template, fold your newspaper in half, draw half a heart, cut it out and then unfold the paper.

- Instead of hanging your hearts in a heart shape, try hanging them at regular intervals along each length of string. It will look just as nice!

- If you can't find a suitable branch, a length of balsawood dowel will work just as well. You can purchase this at any craft store.

Try this

- Paint your branch in coloured stripes. Or, if you prefer a more natural look, leave your branch unpainted.

- Cut two-dimensional hearts from different coloured papers and staple to strings for a quick and easy mobile.

24

DREAMCATCHER

When it comes to making your own dreamcatcher, the possibilities are endless!
Rummage through any craft supplies you have at home to design your unique piece.

Materials: bamboo hoop (purchased at any craft store), ribbons, craft glue, old necklaces, felt, lace doily

Tools: scissors, sewing needle and thread

1. Select a long length of ribbon to cover your hoop. Glue one end of the ribbon onto the hoop and allow to dry.

2. Wrap the ribbon tightly around and around the hoop, until the entire hoop is covered in ribbon. Glue the other end of the ribbon onto the hoop and allow to dry.

3. You will want to decorate approximately the bottom quarter of the hoop. Tie ribbons to the hoop along this quarter, knotting at the back of the hoop, or secure them with a needle and thread or craft glue.

4. Using a needle and thread, attach one end of each of your necklaces to the hoop.

5. Cut feather shapes from the felt, and attach with a needle and thread to the end of the necklaces.

6. Attach your lace doily to the middle of the hoop, using a needle and thread to secure it in place.

7. Ask an adult to help you hang your dreamcatcher.

HINTS

- Make sure you choose a doily for the centre of your hoop that will almost fill your hoop.
- Choose necklaces that have a fastening that can be undone, rather than necklaces on elastic (which will need to be cut).
- For a traditional shape, hang shorter lengths of materials from each side of the hoop, working up to longer pieces in the middle.
- Hang your dreamcatcher in the window or on a glass door so that it will catch the light.
- If you can't find a bamboo hoop, a circular bag handle or an embroidery hoop would also work to form the frame.

Try this

- Hang decorated hoops in descending sizes underneath the main hoop to create a more complex dreamcatcher.
- Attach bells to your dreamcatcher so that it will tinkle in the breeze.
- Decorate your ribbons by gluing on buttons or knotting on beads.

FABRIC WALL HANGINGS

Materials: embroidery hoops of different sizes (purchased at any craft store), fabrics in assorted patterns and colours, nails or permanent mounting tape

Tools: scissors, hammer

Use as many hoops and fabrics as you like to create this fun, elegant wall display.

1. Choose your fabrics and the hoops they will go in. Experiment with patterns, colours and hoop sizes by laying them on the floor and mixing and matching until you are happy with the combination.

2. Unscrew the fastening at the top of your embroidery hoop to separate the two parts of the hoop.

3. Lay the fabric flat over the part of the hoop that forms a complete circle.

4. Place the other part of the hoop on top and push down so the two parts of the hoop are side by side with the fabric secured in between.

5. Make sure the fabric is pulled tight and that you're happy with the section of fabric that is on display.

6. Tighten the fastening at the top of the hoop.

7. Turn your hoop over and carefully trim the fabric that protrudes from between the two pieces of hoop. Trim close to the hoop so that any extra fabric won't be visible from the front.

8. Repeat steps 2 to 7 with your remaining hoops and fabric.

9. Ask an adult to help you hang your hoops on your wall using small nails or permanent mounting tape.

HINTS

- Use an odd number of hoops in a variety of sizes to create a more interesting display.
- Try to choose fabrics in coordinated colours or themes.
- Before you attach your hoops to the wall, work out a layout for your display by positioning your hoops on the floor.

Try this

- Use material from your favourite old T-shirts to give them a second life.
- Varnish your hoops or paint them in different colours and allow to dry before inserting the fabrics.
- If you can't display your hoops on a wall then stand them on a ledge or bookshelf.

STENCILLED BOOKENDS

Use the handy stencils on page 33 & 34, or repurpose a picture from one of your favourite storybooks to create these stencilled bookends.

Materials: two pavers (purchased at most hardware or gardening stores), spray paint in two colours, stencil or picture, sticky tape, double-sided tape

Tools: sandpaper, clean cloth, newspaper, photocopier, scissors

1. Lightly sand your pavers. Wipe away excess dust with a clean cloth.

2. Ask an adult for help with this step. This is best done outside. Place the pavers on newspaper. Choose the colour that you would like your image to be, and spray the pavers with paint in this colour until they are covered completely. Allow to dry.

3. Use the stencil of your choice from page 33 & 34, or, choose an image from one of your books and photocopy it. Enlarge or reduce the image in size so that it will fit onto the front of your paver.

4. Cover the front of the image in sticky tape, and the reverse side in double-sided tape. If you are using a ready-made stencil, just cover the back in double-sided tape. If you are using a photocopied image, carefully cut around your image with scissors.

5. Stick your image or stencil onto one of your pavers.

6. Spray with your second choice of coloured paint until the paver is completely covered. Allow to dry for several minutes before removing your stencil.

7. Repeat the process with the other paver and allow both to dry completely.

HINTS

- Make sure you use spray paint in a well-ventilated area - outside is best.
- Use short puffs of paint rather than spraying continuously to avoid drips.
- Remember that your chosen image will remain in the original paint colour.
- Choose an image that will form a nice, clean silhouette.

Try this

- If you can't find a paver, use a brick or heavy block of wood.
- Instead of photocopying an image, use lace tape, masking tape or stickers to make your stencil design.
- If you don't want to use spray paint, use acrylic paint and a foam roller brush.

To help you on your journey to create your dream room, we've made some handy press-out pieces. Here are a few ideas on how to use them to personalise your space.

STENCILS AND DECORATIVE PRESS-OUT PIECES

Use these stencils for your bookends (page 30), or trace around them to create an instant outline for your potato-print stamp (page 18). Alternatively, you can use the press-out pieces to decorate your jewellery organiser (page 12), or simply as decorations around your room.

PHOTO FRAMES

Stick your favourite photos or images into these frames then tuck them into the elastic on your pinboard (page 22) or peg them on to the strings in your repurposed picture frame (page 20) or insert them into store-bought frames. We've made these frames double sided, so when you're ready for a change, turn them over for a fresh new look!

DOOR HANGING AND DOOR NAMEPLATE

You don't want to be disturbed when you're concentrating on your projects, so let visitors know whose room this is and whether or not you're available with this cute double-sided door hanging and customisable door nameplate. Don't forget to add your name!

BUNTING TEMPLATES AND POMPOM MAKER

Trace around these templates onto decorative paper to create your bunting pieces (page 2). We've also created a pompom maker that you can use when creating your rug (page 6) – wrap yarn around this piece instead of using your hand for super uniform pompoms.

BIRTHDAY CALENDAR

You'll never forget a special birthday again with this useful calendar! Simply write the date and the birthday person's name under each month and display the calendar on your wall. Or, use the other side to keep track of important events.

GOAL LIST AND INSPIRATIONS

Write your goals and reminders on post-it notes, then stick them to this handy chart! Or, use post-it notes on the reverse side to keep track of your favourite quotes or things that inspire you.

LABELS AND STORAGE TAGS

Get organised with these cute labels and storage tags! Simply write on the labels, then attach them to your storage containers, folders or books. These will be useful when you're desk decorating (page 8) or on any storage boxes in your room.

STENCILS
AND
DECORATIVE
PRESS-OUT
PIECES

PHOTO
FRAMES

35

PHOTO
FRAMES

36

PHOTO
FRAMES

PHOTO
FRAMES

Door hanging and door nameplate

COME IN
- I'm free

Lives Here

Lives Here

Door hanging and door nameplate

SHHH
- I'm busy

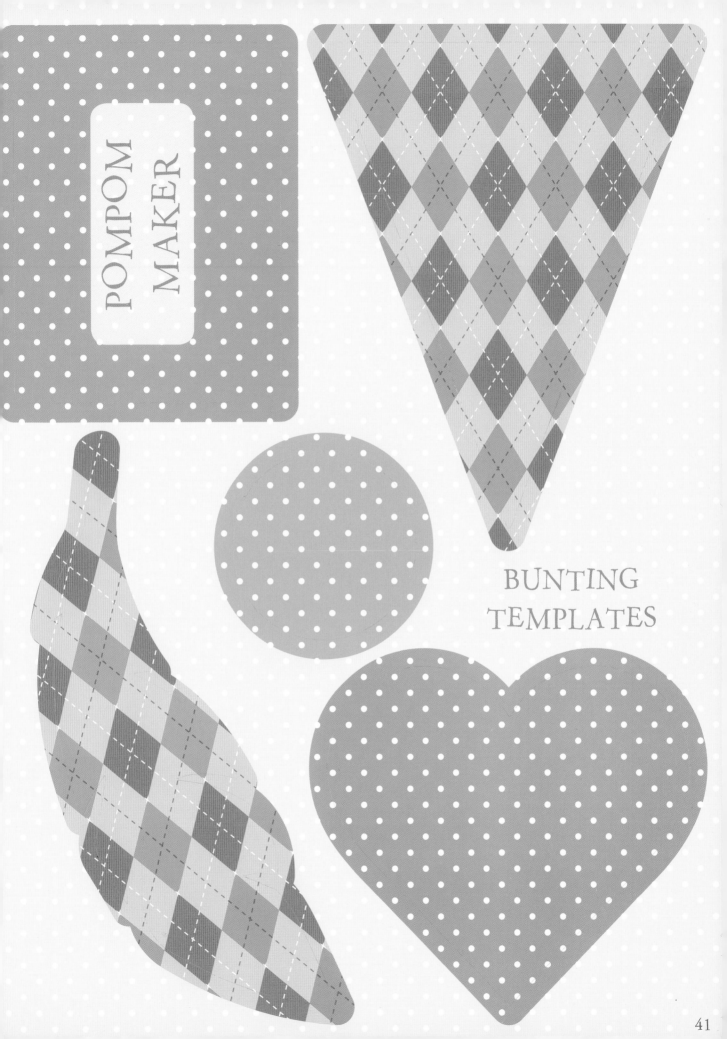

POMPOM MAKER

BUNTING
TEMPLATES

POMPOM
MAKER

BUNTING
TEMPLATES

Special Birthdays

January

February

March

April

May

June

July

August

September

October

November

December

Special Events

January	February	March

April	May	June

July	August	September

October	November	December

MY GOALS

Quotes and Inspirations

Mistakes are proof that you are trying
– Anonymous

Life does not have to be perfect to be wonderful
– Annette Funicello

LABELS AND
STORAGE
TAGS

LABELS AND
STORAGE
TAGS